Fat Girl Finishing School

by **RACHEL WILEY**

Wiley, Rachel
1st edition.
ISBN: 978-0-989-0092-2-5

Edited by Ariana Brown
Proofread by Ariana Brown
Cover and interior layout design by Amy McDonnold

Printed in Tennessee, USA

Timber Mouse Publishing
Austin, TX
www.timbermouse.com

To contact the author, please email rachielouwho@gmail.com.

*"I am so beautiful, sometimes people weep when they see me.
And it has nothing to do with what I look like really, it is just that
I gave myself the power to say that I am beautiful, and if I could
do that, then maybe there is hope for them too. And the great
divide between the beautiful and the ugly will cease to be.
Because we are all what we choose."*
~ Margaret Cho

CONTENTS

PRE–FLIGHT PRAYER OF A FAT GIRL

Pray, let us be thankful for the well trained smile of the flight attendant
it may be the only one pointed at us on this day.
Let us not be embarrassed to request the seat belt extender
but rather rejoice in its being.
Let us pray for a seat that sits not on an aisle
but a window so we may cling to the plane wall
in attempt to make ourselves small
enough
Let us also move our bodies as little as possible enduring cramp and ache alike
so as not to be a burden unto our seatmate.
And blessed be that seatmate who does neither sigh nor scorn
when our hip sneaks over the line of the armrest
Yay, let us never book with SouthWest for they will send us into exile
for not being fruitful and purchasing 2 seats to contain our bounty when only 1
    can be afforded.
Pray, let us ignore the glances when the pilot announces the craft is overweight
and must sit flightless while luggage is rearranged for balance.
Lo, let us not look to the magazine models tucked into the seat backs like hymnals
as anything holy
Pray, let us remember we are beautiful in our bounty
Pray most of all that we forgive ourselves
And smooth the creases of apology we have folded our delicate bodies into on
    this day
Come home and stretch out across our beds like the unpacking of a suitcase full
    of all the best souvenirs.
Our bones are racks of the kitschiest key chains.
Our bellies, magnificent snow globes.
Look and rejoice at everything we managed to get home safe.

ODE TO TRACY TURNBLAD

Ode to my first fat role model,
Fat rolls modeled
Patron Saint of Fat Girl Rebellion
Ode to swinging hips wide while doing the watoosie.
of being both the fat friend AND the love interest
Kissing the cute boy on screen without an ounce of unworth
Ode to your chubby hands and their take
Ode to your deserving
Your unsettling
Your twist and shout trail blazing
Ode to taking the mean girl's lunch
and her boyfriend
and still having time to spray your hair high
and fight like an ally
Ode to that dress in the last scene of the film
that pink silk sheath of defiance...
with a train!
Ode to your royal drag queen mother for turning arch eyebrow to bar raised,
for stuffing all of her decadent orbit into those pencil skirts
Ode to my own mother for gifting you to me a VHS hymnal
when I was 8 years old
and so chubby
and learning how to pray in my own temple.

AMERICANA

I am 16 years old at a party full of rebel yell and Pabst Blue Ribbon
a boy/girl party where we have all come in search of that piece of Americana
found only when teenagers are left unattended and the liquor cabinet unlocked.
Where we learn how to drink ourselves more courageous than our insecurities.

On the floor of an upstairs bedroom
there is a boy sliding his hand up my thigh,
a smile dangling from his bottom lip like a lit cigarette
he looks at me full moon eyed dreamy
presses his whole body into my whole body
tells me I am "the prettiest half breed he has ever seen"

1 hour earlier,
this confederate flag of a boy loudly announced that he would not be playing
    any of that
"nigger music"
and before his throat could kick the chair from under the R
I bottle smash my manners,
tell him whose daughter I am
threaten to show him just how black I could be if he dare say it again.
He does not know that my face is a two way mirror
that I am a speakeasy only old black women on the city bus ever really know
    the knock to,
they recognize the taboo tearing at the edges of my light skin and fine hair.
In the summer I am the color of hot church gossip when the sun burns brown
    into my cheeks.
My spine is a railroad tie on the tracks that segregate the races in my mother's
    pink cheeked southern Ohio town
I am only a girl who knows this word is flint to the gunpowder in her blood
but still trips over the trigger when trying to explain why you can't say it.
He may well just be a boy repeating a word dribbled from his father's chin like
    so much Skoal
but he is already easing into the luxury of never having to worry about the kickback.

The party has boiled down to a drunken murmur of unhooking bras.
This boy stumbles onto the refuge I have made of the last empty room in the house
where I have long given up on playing Americana.
It is on the floor of this darkened bedroom he pushes my hair from my eyes
cradles my olive face in his soft pink palm
and leans his mouth so close to my mouth.
I am both aware and not aware that he is not calling me pretty
that he is calling me *close enough*.
I want to tell you how I set fire to this boy's lawn
I want to tell you how I renamed him and denied his history
I want to tell you how I shoved this passing right down his throat
Instead I am left to consider the 14 years I spent pretending
that I didn't let him kiss me anyway.

PURPLE HEARTS

The night my 87 year old Great Grandmother died
she was coming home from a date
but
wet pavement
and
impractical shoes
a broken hip
a body in shock
a passing

The first time I ever heard the word slut
it kettle steam slipped from between the plastic pearl veneers of my Aunt Delores
as a procession of antique soldiers in their dressiest dress blues from the VFW,
where my Mamaw gave out warm plates and warmer hands to troops of empty
   housed men,
filed one after another
dropping the contents of their left breast pockets into the box where my Grandmother lay
beautiful in too much rouge,
delicate like some ancient corsage
and I decided that someday I want to be a slut
just like Grandma
and be sent up to glory on a parade of grateful, unlonelied hearts.

WHAT BETTE DAVIS MADE ME DO

1962 Bette Davis in too much rouge and a baby doll dress
lives in the upstairs apartment in my head
an awful tenant
she vacillates between
draped serene across my skull
and a piano key cyclone
banging out a trapped pigeon symphony
against the walls and windows.

She steers all of the laughter to my back
charges a nickel for a peek at my naked and aging fingers.
Bette Davis pedal pushes the crank of my jaw
an insecure gramophone
apologizing for all of the broken glass in my feet
and the bloody dance step diagram I've left on the good rug
She runs the well-meaning neighbors from the porch with a glare and cackle
and shouts all of the fire flies down from the sky.

She is a booming voice demand
at the top of the stairs
That I stop my sniveling
She stands ready
with loaded hands to the small of my back.
tells me how I would make such a lovely spill
as I am made up of the most triumphant waste.

Every time she makes a run for my fingernails
I change the locks
but Bette Davis is crafty squatter
knows where all the loose floorboards are.
My love is a match maker
threatens to her smoke her out
wedges match sticks up my spine
she quiets at the smell of sulfur
I am a beautiful fire risk.
He is a patient burn victim just waiting to happen.

LOVE LETTER TO MY BODY # 3: MY EXCUSE

in response to "Fit Mom" Maria Kang

My excuse is pumpkin ice cream and 3 seasons of Luther on Netflix.
...is that corn dogs go great with a side of feelings
...is that I actually really like the two little dimples right above my big fat ass
...is that I have no children and therefore get all of the cookies
...is what better way to celebrate a negative diabetes test than with a
   muthafuckin cupcake
...is sleeping in and good pillows
...is the knowledge that if you eat a piece of dark chocolate and take a drink of
   red cream soda it tastes like a cherry cordial
...is that they make pretty dresses in size Unexcused these days
...is, even if they didn't I would sew three of yours together and wear it 3 times
   better than you ever did
...is that I had 2 ice cream bars and an orgasm for breakfast this morning, come
   at me!
My excuse is that my body needs no excuse to be loved
No excuse to be seen
No excuse to be touched, enjoyed, celebrated
I will not excuse my body unless of my hip or breast should brush your body
when we cross paths
but, if we're being honest, a you're welcome is more likely in order
It's okay to want a piece, Maria
No excuse.

HOW TO BECOME A HERETIC

"It is harder to get out than to stay out" ~ *Mark Twain*

Even though the house is emptier than you planned
you are still tip toeing through it,
a swarm of telltale eggshells scuttling under foot.
The voices in the kitchen having all gone to gossip,
a cackle of smudgeless faces upturned to heaven.
You are petty burglar on a Sunday morning
coaxing down a flock of frightened prayers from the hall closet,
tucking them safely behind your teeth.
This is how it feels right before you become a heretic
and must leave for the last time with only what you can fit into your pockets
the boxes packed and smuggled out the back door
one by one in secret over weeks and the passing of plagues,
the china swaddled in newspaper
for the husband they deemed you too heathen for
and served your ringless fingers
to a woman of softer teeth
and stronger faith.
The blankets all left in a solemn herd
when they gave away your children
and reproached you for your vacant womb.
A steeple with no bell, they called you.
Each one of the kitchen knives slid under the door
when you felt a congregation of arms
unwinding from your unrepentant frame,
the unknitting of the most pious sweater.
At last your great grandmother's 45's rode out on your hips
when the fire in your chest
that you named faith
but they called devil
kept setting off the smoke alarm
so you take that too
for its screeching and honest tambourine song.
This is why God sounds like evacuation to you
Why tongues heavy in gold leaf are not to be trusted
Why you can stand on valleys of angry match heads
in bare feet
without flinching
This is what it feels like to become a heretic
a churchless hymnal
a hungry and blasphemous child.

SHUTTER

We take photographs of ourselves in downward angles
because we like the way the gods see us.
Posed photographs are not real.
It never happened,
you were not there.
Candid shots hold still everything
we are trying to shake our tadpole tails away from without ever having learned
    to swim.

Film based photographs used to be taken of lowly men and handsome women
just the same as starlets and heroes
developed in the same solutions.
The pan tipped gently back and forth in the dark
Liquid slither
over and back
Until faces appear
over and back
Until you could see the souls in their eyes.
over and back
all glossy
all Kodak stamped for assurance.

No one is saving baby pictures from burning buildings anymore
it's all made to cut and run
to edit out those lowly men
those handsome women
Everyone the starlet
Everyone the hero
built on altars on tubes and metal

We take photographs in downward angles
The way the Gods see us
Dead eyed and deletable
worship who we want to be
Not lowly men, never lowly men
Never handsome women
we are creatures vain and squirming
uncomfortable in gun smoke flash outside our own hands
uncomfortable in the heat of bulb
Uncomfortable in the click and spin of film
Soldiers go to war and die with empty breast pockets
No one is saving photographs while cities burn
We offer instead as tinder that fat around our faces
That slightly lazy eye
And that bump in your nose along with all of its ugly history.

GORGON

Fashion designer, Karl Lagerfeld thinks himself modern Perseus
Damns us all of soft shape into Snake Haired Gorgon
then beheads us.
Decrees from high atop Mount Fashion Week
With a laugh in his throat and the shake of his head.
No one wants to see round women.

Television stations refuse to air commercials for a plus size lingerie line
says the model has too much cleavage to be deemed appropriate for tv
names her *Titan*
expels her into the abyss.
This model is too much

We are too much
We are inappropriate
We should really do something about it
embrace glossy magazine stacked pedestals to the back of our throats
retch to fit atop them
without wobbling
threat of airbrush gun to the head if they wobble.
Beauty, it fits between the margins.

We are too much
We are not enough
We are not people
but punch lines
head shakes
tongue clicks
such a shame
such a waste
such a pretty face
rolled up smacked on the nose with collarbones
stay off the furniture
silly girl, no sitting on the loveseat
Beauty, it fits between the armrests

You are too fat to fly
wings clipped
the sky belongs to Zeus
You have thunder thighs
and not enough lightning.
You are too much
You are not enough
You are a disruption
You are an insecurity risk.
Every hissing hair on your head too defiant
The part of the story so often lost is that Medusa
was born so beautiful
made ugly by another's demand.
Mr. Lagerfeld,
Is it so much easier to make us monsters
than to simply make us dresses?
If you promise to lower your sword
and look at me,
Really look at me
I promise I won't turn you into stone.

LOVE LETTER TO MY BODY # 7

In Honor of National Coming Out Day

dear body today more than any day let us smile and remember the excited rush of blood to cheeks the first time we kissed a woman full passion and familiar the way she and I did not take or push or expect but gave and gave and gave how my hands shook not with fear but with joy of touching skin so home the way she and I turned quickly a seamless figure of giggle and kiss in the bathroom of the bar that damned broken lock on the stall door that exposed us again and again that glorious broken lock on the stall door for reminding us again and again that we were doing nothing at all wrong

PROOF

The first time in seven years I saw you coming
I smoothed down my wild hair
leveled hems
hid tooth razored cuticles.
I wanted you to know that I am at best okay,
a choreographed apology,
a straightening up
for that autumn I spent as a house fire on your front lawn
smoke rolling spoonful thick from my mouth
the contents of the attic tossed flaming from the windows
into your lap

Before your shoulder could pass mine on the sidewalk
I shook my hour glass throat down to last grain
trying to tell you everything
I really miss telling you everything
pretty sure you were the last faithful listener
tuned into the static of dying air
while the glowing light
of my console radio chest dimmed

I did not know until you had gone
that you may as well have been stuffed with dry leaves
Your spine a bookshelf of rare first editions
I understand now that you could not enlist
I should have never tried to carve arches into your feet

I need you to know,
I am more water than smoke now
more jitterbug jukebox than front line friendly fire
and despite the years of silence and the fact that our hearts found other homes
I will want to kiss your mouth
to prove all of this to you.

CONVERSATIONS WITH MY FATHER IN A DUNK TANK

When you met my mother
was she all the best parts of the soil
and all the brightest spots in the sky?
Did she kiss from you the ember warm ashes
of fires long burnt out?
Do you remember when your love turned attic trapped bird
and started slamming its own feathers out against the windows
wild eyed
and desperate?

She warned me to run from men with treble clef heart lines
but someone went and stole the guts
from the player piano in my chest
now its just a
piano
I have to make up the songs
work the pedals on my own
some days when my toes don t quite touch
I rent the space to a boy with longer legs
and nimble fingers
he can read sheet music, Dad
it fills my mouth with buck shot music notes
He smells like first love
I would run through myself to get away
but I am no runner.

The empty refrigerator in my stomach
wants to know where Florida is
and if we are there yet
and if when we get there
we will find all of the runaway fathers
living under dining room table forts
sitting on thrones of unmailed birthday cards.
We never changed our number, Dad.

It still rings to the same black wall mounted telephone
that hung in the last house we all lived in together.
It was sole witness
to the day the roof above the kitchen fell in on Mom.
Did you hear about that?
Did you worry?
I bet you didn't know that the crane that came to fix it
rolled right over the parsley patch I tended to.
We never have been very good at growing things
When I was the same age you and she were at the end
I moved out of a garden meant to grow nice Christian girls
into good Christian housewives.
I walked off one day with no shoes
the taste of glass and feathers in my mouth.
I understand a few things about leaving now, Dad.

I don't remember you going
only the way mom started saying "father" through her jawbone
until we stopped asking where you
or Florida were anymore.
I learned how to walk in eggshell roller skates
with Janis Joplin giving her heart away
shaking the windows like a low flying airplane
and I grew up
looking a whole lot
like nobody in particular.

BRASS KNUCKLES
After Lauren Zuniga/ For my best friend Desiree Pipenger

My very smart friend Lauren says that if we name things they become less scary.
So let's name the rest of this year the year of not settling for anymore of this
    basic ass shit.
The year of "fuck you! We're amazing!"
The year of not apologizing
(even without words)
for things outside our control
like snoring
or being amazing,
or flirting with that cute bartender
or kissing that beautiful woman.
for being self-sufficient and battle scarred and calloused knuckle
and still standing;
the year we learn,
though they are not as perfect as we so often expect mothers to be,
our mothers were not wrong about everything;
after all they are still standing too.
The year of knowing our own hearts well enough
to know how to wedge our thumb into the cracks and break them apart
of knowing that sometimes we really have to just go ahead
and wedge our thumbs into the cracks and break them apart
like pulling the rip cord on a parachute
cause we know the taste of ground
and it tastes too much like settling.
So, maybe we got lost and showed up late to the party for people who can
change the world
but we're here and there's still plenty of dip left.
We will name this *The Year We Gave the Horizon a Black Eye for all its Back-Talk*
and Lived 3 Hard Lives to tell About It.
We'll call it *The Year of Brass Knuckles* for short.
The year of knuckle down,
the year of whoever never told you that you are everything
is fucking liar
and there's no room for liars on this ship.

No sir.
This here is The SS Knuckle Duster
We are the captains
We are the wind
the bounty
and the water
we are the siren song
we are full steam ahead
we are not getting smaller
we are done getting smaller
we are meeting the horizon line to tell it our demands.
We are brass knuckle lovely and we are not done yet
No, we are not done yet
We.
Are
Not.
Done.
Yet.

We aren't even close.

DEMETER

America,
I birthed you a daughter once.
You did not let me name her.
Instead, you taught her to answer to the cat calls
of men shoving fistfuls of dollar bills into her panties.
Taught her if she keeps the wig on
and her top off
They will call her *Right, Idol*, some kind of truth
Trade her grace that is not theirs to give away
for choices that are not theirs to make.

In the pink glimmer of sunrise each morning
I call to her
I call her Persephone
...Eve
..Susan, Lucretia, Elizabeth
...Adrienne, Shirley, Betty, Gloria, Audre
I call her Woman
beg her apple skin eyes open
mourn her swollen belly
and the razor mouthed sons she will birth for you one day.

America,
I would sooner fill my hips with dynamite
before I ever gave her to you again.

*"It remains a radical act to be fat and happy in America...
Being publically fat and happy is hard; being publically, shamelessly,
unshakably fat and happy is an act of both will and bravery"*
~ Melissa McEwan

THIS IS JUST TO SAY
After William Carlos Williams

This is Just to Say
I have eaten
the beauty standards
that were in
the icebox
and which you were probably
clinging to
for profit
Forgive me
they were ridiculous
so binding
and so cold.

3 HEART MONTY

I was born with a hole in my heart
it does not hurt until someone slips through it
not the way punches hurt
but the way failure hurts
the way I imagine the spaghetti strainer might feel
when it lets a noodle slip through despite its very best efforts at being a
    spaghetti strainer.
If I was born with a giant squid heart
which is to say
if I had three hearts
(which I might)
I would tell you that 1 of them
is always occupied by one boy
sometimes he occupies a full 2 of them
but right now it's only 1
because I am too sensitive
and he is too forgetful
but I could never stay mad at him
because I know too much of his story.
His story, it makes me wish I was a magician
I would turn one of my hearts into a dove
and set him free
but that magic is all slight off hand
and I am honest like fluorescent lights on white tile floors
so I will just love him and hope it's worth something like having feathers
but this is all just to say that could still love you
also
The third heart is always open
like a diner car in St Paul, Minnesota
people revolve in and out of it
sometimes they come back for a whole week at a time
pick a spot and name it theirs
sometimes they dine and dash
I wait so much longer than I should
to see if they will come back.
If you told me that you would come back
and meant it
and then actually came back
I could probably give you a whole heart
all your own
if you wanted it
but I will warn you
it has a hole in it.

10 HONEST THOUGHTS ON BEING LOVED BY A SKINNY BOY

1. I say," I am fat."
He says, "No, you are beautiful"
I wonder why I cannot be both.
He kisses me
hard.

2. My college theater professor once told me
That despite my talent
I would never be cast as a romantic lead
We put on plays that involve flying children
And singing animals
but apparently
no one has enough willing suspension of disbelief
to buy anyone loving a fat girl

3. On the mornings I do not feel pretty,
While he is still asleep,
I sit on the floor and check the pockets of his skinny jeans for a motive
for a punchline
for other girls' phone numbers

4. When we hold hands in public
I wonder if he notices the stares
like he is handling a parade balloon
down a crowded sidewalk
I wonder if he notices
how my hands are made of rope.

5. Dear Cosmo
Fuck you!
I will not take your sex tips
on how to please a man
you do not think my body will ever be worthy of

6. He tells me he loves me,
with the lights on.
7. I can cup his hip bone in the palm of my hand
Feel his ribs without pressing very hard at all
Sip wine from his collarbones
He does not believe me when I tell him he is beautiful.
Sometimes I fear the day he does
is the day he leaves.

8. The cute hipster girl at the coffee shop assumes we are just friends
And flirts across the counter
I spend the next two weeks replacing my face with hers
In all of our photographs.
When I finally admit this
We spend the whole night taking pictures
He will not let me delete a single one

9. The phrase "Big Girls need Love too" can go die in a fire.
Fucking me does not require an asterisk.
Loving me is not a fetish.
Finding me beautiful is not a novelty.
I am not a fucking novelty.

10. I say, "I am fat."
He says, "No, you are so much more"
and He kisses me
Hard.

VENOM

When the ER doctor says the words venomous spider bite
as he pinches the purple mass spreading across your calf
the next logical diagnosis can only be
death, amputation, or super powers.
So, when the doctor sends you home unnerved
with a round of "preventative antibiotics"
you are resting assured that he is basically saying
Enjoy your web slinging, crime fighting future my friend!

On the way to the pharmacy
you stroll past a mugging
and barely contain your joy
because you know that soon
so very soon
you will get to serve up justice to scum bags like that
becoming a hero to innocent citizens
like that poor bleeding women you just stepped over.
She will look to you with hope and thanks brimming over in her eyes,
you will smile modestly
and be on your way to further better this grimy world we live in.
You will be rewarded with keys to the city,
homage in the form of childhood Halloween costumes
and SEX!
No one group of people can possibly get more freaky
than a bunch recently rescued and grateful citizens, amiright?

During the stomach cramping and diarrhea that follow the next 3 days
you assume these to be minor growing pains
that come with the transition from mild mannered to super
and have nothing to do with the enormous antimicrobial
and antifungal resistance you are downing 6 times per day everyday
Soon you'll be fighting evils so much bigger than unquilted toilet paper!

By the 6th day
your comic book panels are a shattered stained glass of disappointment
when you realize how you've been trick-or-treating-Charlie-Brown fucked
when the antibiotics went all symbiote on your vagina
and in place of web slinging action
you have been left with a yeast infection.

You've traded the ability to produce silken webs from your wrists
for the ability to produce yeast
so much yeast
from your vagina.

Your yeast will never rise to any occasion.
Never take across the skyline in pursuit of madmen
and bank robbers.
Your secret identity shifts from Rouge Photo Journalist
to Woman Pretending She Doesn't Have a Fucking Yeast Infection.
No costume tights hiding under your day to day clothing
only itching
and shame
Your arch nemesis nothing more than a faulty applicator in the Monostat 7 box.
There are no keys to the city
No kid wants to be YeastWoman for Halloween
There will be no burning buildings full of beautiful grateful people
to assuage the burning in your pants
because as is clearly stated
3 times
in bold
on the Monostat box
there will definitely be no sex
no glory, no hope for this city.
You quietly curse Peter Parker for his lucky accident
and adjust the applicator
yet again.

LOVE LETTER TO MY BODY # 8: INKED

Dear Body,
Look at all this space we've got!
Look at all of this blank canvas just waiting for ink.
I got big plans to roll our skin in fat girl pin-ups
and cupcakes
and war cries
and defiant pachyderms
to wear my big fat heart on my big fat sleeve
and dare anyone to call it a target
to then sit and watch the lines soften with age
until you are a smudged sidewalk chalk mural of still here.

HOARDER

In Texas there is a woman who let despair eat her whole house.
Built a mausoleum of dime store romance novels
on her late husband's side of the bed.
The bed they shared for over 30 years.
This mausoleum had to be dismantled by strangers with snow shovels
after the neighbors complained about the strong stench of sorrow
wafting from the house on a high wind
and the way it lowered their property value.
How could she let it get so bad?

The widow stands on her porch in a daze
wearing an apologetic smile
as dumpster after dumpster is filled with her bone marrow
and hauled away.

Halfway through the cleanup,
under a stack of paperback harlot heaving bosoms
they find a mummified copperhead snake frozen mid strike.
The widow's until then estranged daughter holds it out in quaking hands
says, *Mom, do you understand, this could have killed you?*
The widow only nods
and smiles
Her eyes spilling over with *if only.*
She is long gone.

They don't notice our deaths sometimes
until we have all but burst at the seams
until we are a neighborhood blight
an impending foreclosure
a bloated corpse.

FOR NICHOLAS WHO IS SO CONCERNED

The band was full swing the night we met
My beautiful all cotton pressed and petticoat full
You lead me away from the dance floor
concern bruising the top of my arm
to remind me,
in an embarrassed whisper,
that I am much too fat
and making a fool of myself
with all of this skin I wear
all of this immodest self love
all of this space I am taking
and still taking.

My God, people are watching.
Don't I know I am dying
Don't I know I am a sugar blooded elephant
O' Nicholas
Forgive my clumsy audacity in forgetting to hate my tusks
I was so dangerously carefree
Who knows what could have happened
I might have incited a herd of gray fleshed wallflowers
to shake the chandeliers down to the floor
with the sound of skin smack
and hip sway
and unapologetic buoyance
Thank goodness you were there
to lead me home
your insecurities
binding my wayward trunk

I am obviously a large and simple girl,
and left home without my own
stumbled into feeling all too human
with the air kissing my unsightly skin

I have forgotten my place
like I never felt laughter slinky walk my spine
or deep kissed pavement at an insult backfired from a passing car
or felt every single knuckle in a punch line
You would think I'd have learned by now
that this body
and its fault lines
do not belong to me
My fat
a crime scene of other people's concern
I seem to swallow everything
so why not your good intentions too?

A little known fact about elephants and rooms:
everyone sees the elephant standing there
they all think they are the first to point her out
the first to tell her she is an elephant
the elephant is very aware she is an elephant
by nature does not forgot this
the room would never allow her to forget this
so she may as well dance
Take your bull hook hands off me
I am no one's broken beast
and I've got whole houses to shake down
to clapboard and brick dust.

TRAGEDY

They used to call us *tragedies*
for the Negro blood running underground
beneath safe house skin
1 drop
they said,
sure to drive us mad with mixed up impurity.
a tell tale heart of have
slamming against the service entrance of have not
skin the color of survivors guilt
We hands over gasping mouths
lest we give ourselves away to be hanged too.
We tragedies.

Now they count us mile markers
on the road to some ivory bricked post racial promised land
A utopia
Where Jim Crow is a blue eyed tweeting sparrow
Where nigger is not offensive but to call someone a racist is.
Where privilege does not wipe her feet
but shows up to your house on Halloween
wearing your history smeared across her face
a burnt cork and bleeding joke.
A flickering white flame
inside a carved out Aunt Jemima
Informs us that it is time, now, to laugh at this.
Dances to the sound of our hearts
banging against the floor boards
Chides us to lower our voice
before we know we're screaming
Reminds us to know our place
before we drag the whole party down
Tells us the burning cross on the front lawn
is a bonfire.
Warm up to this.

The house may well have been completely submerged
for all the underwater scream I was that night
the party guests a smack of absent minded water lilies
posing for pictures proud as any lynching day postcard
while I stumbled out of my own house scrapping mud from behind my teeth

There have been too many fathers buried in poplar tree neck ties
too many mothers in hangmen's pearls
for me to be run from my own home
for me to laugh at the corpse this privileged girl has split open
and worn like a party dress
for me to quiet the rhythm in my blood
for me to still be a tragedy.
to be anything less than a screaming revolt.

LOVE LETTER TO MY BODY # 10

A love note from one body to another

Dear Body,

I feel the way you go all firework at the sight of them all tight muscled so as not to waterfall awkard at their feet, the way your eye contact turns the way of loosed balloon strings, your throat becomes a curious but shy child words peeking from your coy smile mouth. If our heart were something more brave-our hands could write them a love note that says something like:

Your hips are the loveliest fleet of dreamboats. Your sketchbook skin reads like my favorite fairytale. You bring the flashlights and I will build us one palace of a blanket fort. Meet me in Nebraska.

PADLOCK'S DAUGHTER

After the street light whispers died down
And the neighbor boy with bent hair pin fingers was sent away
I woke up broken in a house full of padlocks
Stood in the empty hallway
Swallowing fistfuls of skeleton keys,
Begging forgiveness,
Twisting myself combination
Two clicks to the right past what the neighbors might think
Three clicks to the left past promising this would never happen again
Scratch the numbers from the dial
Constructed alters of dead bolts in my stomach
Tried to rebuild myself a fortress.

Before any of this my mother would often wonder aloud
Whether or not I could actually be hers
As I had not inherited her peephole eyes
Or barred window smile
And now here I stood
Banging on her door
With bolt cutter scars down my thighs
As proof that was made of some softer metal
That I could not possibly have come from her
A vault would never birth something so weak
So giving
So breakable

A POEM FOR AMY WINEHOUSE

I could never do what you did girl
never sing girl
swallowed sidewalk and iron gate
let their jagged edge drag down all the soft spaces
hoped to cough up some Billie Holiday soul
ended up with blood and spit in my hands
never bead strung notes from the gravel in my palms girl
not like you
never so blue girl
never so black and blue girl
not like you
they'll say they saw you going girl

but they sure never saw you coming

When that humming bird moved into your heart
it was because you were holding nectar girl
sweet slow soul dripping nectar in your chest girl
Your throat shouldn't have known how to sing whiskey like that girl
record needle between the toes like you girl
your grooves they fit me girl
They swung me girl
bloomed orchids in my lungs girl
Your ribs whining cemetery gates
Howling ghosts and singing shovels girl
Girl they'll say they saw you going

I could never do what you did girl
Never reach with my vocal cords
tentacle grasping at air for busted heart understanding
for applause girl.
for *you are pretty* girl.
for *you are enough* girl.
for someone to hold you in place from dissolving girl.
never so much broken glass in the hinge of my jaw girl
not like you girl
Girl they'll say they say you going.

I'm sorry your nets only pulled dead fish with flash bulb eyes
to take pictures of you failings girl
to photograph your razor blade collarbones girl
to zoom in on the tube tracks in your arms girl
I'm sorry they made you a silent film with separate soundtrack girl
Girl they're saying they saw you going
So blue girl
So very very blue
I could never sing like you girl
and I never did see you going.

GLASS HALF FULL

After you broke up with me I took off to do what most girls do no matter how
    stereotypical and drown my sorrows in a tub of double fudge chocolate swirl
    ice cream with brownie bits
only my plan was foiled when I missed the last bus leaving the super market
and the double fudge swirl ice cream melted on the long walk home
because I may or may not have spent 20 to 30 minutes longer than necessary
    following a man
who may or may not have looked a great deal like Ira Glass,
attempting to covertly take his picture with my camera phone.
I was planning to send it to you with a message proclaiming him the stone cold
    fox we agreed him to be in the first conversation we ever had.
I thought you would've gotten a laugh out of it and we don't laugh together
    anymore.
I followed him discreetly down the cereal aisle and was sort of disappointed
when he chose Cheerios over Life.
I followed him through the frozen foods right past the frozen veggies
where you once demanded a kiss and tasted a little like Chai Tea.
I lost him briefly when I saw there was a new flavor of Wheat Thins
but at 4.95 a box I quickly re focused and relocated Mr. Glass a couple aisles over.
I only abandoned my mission when I suspected "Ira" was onto me
he turned to look at me
and I in turn pretended to be very interested in the closest item in the aisle but
    found myself rather unfortunately placed in from of a shelf of Depends
and could then only think Oh dear God, Ira Glass now thinks I wear adult diapers!
Was I doomed to become a prologue to a show about incontinence in 3 acts?
And as I am writing this poem at work
I realize that I just looked up the word incontinence on google
to make sure it was in fact the correct word
And if my boss checks my web history
like I think he does
than he now thinks I am incontinent as well!
Unfortunately there is only evidence to support this theory
as I do excuse myself to the restroom several times each day
to cry
because I hate my job and our picture isn't on my desk anymore to remind me not to.

As I walked home the other night carrying what was rapidly becoming a very
    large double fudge swirl milkshake with brownie bits
I switched on my ipod to find that the latest episode of *This American Life*
was all about Reuniting in 3 acts
and I realized that while I knew
even as I stalked him through the grocery store
that this man was not Ira Glass
you may still be the man that I think you are
and this may or may not be the end for us but rather a break between acts.

THERE USED TO BE A FOTOMAT HERE

On the eve of your wedding
I sat feet swinging from a sky line
in a city with an electric gasoline North Star
passing a glass bottom brown bag to a girl resting her head on my hip
mistaking the web between my thumb and forefinger for a lemon wedge
while I say Ohio like it is someplace exotic
making believe we aren't a state of submarines in above ground swimming pools
in someone's front yard,
or that we don't forget so often how far postcards can travel,
or that there are organs other than the heart.

What I am trying to say is that I am sorry
for all that time I spent trying to conjure you back from tail lights
Its just that I had to see the ocean
before I could stop listening for your keys in my front door
Only thick salt and fish scales can smooth away something like
Christmas morning in your maroon Buick
staircase clamoring down snow dusted Indiana highways to introduce me to
    your parents
I should've seen the foreshadowing when the car died
and I had to come home without you
that you would not love me past Easter
much less until my bones begin to shake like fine furniture stacked much too high
and I start demanding to be taken to supermarket chains that don't even exist
    anymore
I wanted to love you like a landmark
Now you will just be some Fotomat
I will swear used to be on the corner of Broadmoore and 11th
but no one else seems to remember
Now you will be North Star for the girl you kissed under the Willow tree
and I will be happy for you

I will write you a wedding toast on a crumpled brown bag
head back to my mid-west Valentine
where there is a boy waiting for my postcard palms free of your exhaust
A boy, who doesn't know what a Fotomat is
but who loves me like guitar strings
like slow dancing in parking lots
like carving early morning hours into eden
A boy I will finally change the locks and love back
like Christmas lights in July
like unfolded maps
A boy I will love like the ocean salt still clinging to my hair.

SUNDAY MORNING CASINO SERVICE

Let us pray to the Bingo hall Gods
and open our wallets to hymn 21
while the slot machine choir sing hymns of fallen coins
into collection plate palms
before raising their arms toward heaven once again
each temple blessed with a harem of Madonnas
haloed in cigarette smoke
oxygen running through their holy rosaries.
Blessed be the poker table confessions
their sacrament given hand over hand
and melt $100 chips on their tongues
the body
sipping complimentary gin
the blood.
Luck is nothing more than Faith rolled in body glitter
wearing a blonde wig and working her way through school.
She'll settle down one of these days.
make someone a good wife

In 1916 Mary the Elephant was hanged from an industrial crane for the murder of her inexperienced trainer. While being stripped of her ivory it was discovered that she'd had 2 abscessed teeth on the side of her face where the trainer repeatey struck her with the bull hook.

THE CIRCUS FAT LADY EULOGIZES
MARY THE ELEPHANT

They've gone and made you a ghastly ornament of uncontrol, Mary.
Your pain overturning a whole city atop the man who dared to handle you
like some dumb creature.
Your largesse
both your attraction and your charge
Isn't it something,
the way these small souled people toss their hard earned nickels at our feet
to marvel at our vastness
to be in the presence of our *dangerous*
to mock their fears in our content
to provoke our great mass into motion so they can crown themselves movers of mountains
worshiping and damning us in 1 breath for the wonders that we are.
Their message clear:
if you cannot be small at least make it easy to handle you
your anger, Mary
our anger, Mary
it reminds them of the ways we can undo them with half the effort
How dare you want for the gentleness reserved for pretty little things
how dare you be so beastly when they only meant to beat you grateful.

And look,
they've gone all drunk on bad justice hauled you into the sky a thunder cloud,
named themselves the Gods of your demise,
robbed your gravestone face with hacksaws for all the trouble of your unrest
how quickly they forget the monumental hearts that drive these monstrous bodies
It took an entire mob and a railroad crane to give them their pound of flesh
and still you gave them tons
Mary, You are survived by all things large and wild hearted and irreproachable
I survive you
I survive you in every beastly enchantment I can muster.

HOME WRECKER

You had always rolled your eyes at the home wreckers on tv talk shows
and their defense that it *just sort of happened.*
You cannot know what that means
until it does
just sort of happen.

A man
A friend
Sits upright one minute
Sinks into you
Erects an altar in thick breath and secrets onto your sternum

You cannot stop your arms from cradling his head
Pushing fingers thru his hair
Pressing lips to his temple
Promise to forgive yourself for it
this first time
Promise you'll be less judgmental of women on television
with the running mascara and shame weighing their heads towards their laps
because you like the way this man gamble roulette spins you
watches your dress fly up around you
his wedding ring bouncing in the pleats.

"A cultural fixation on female thinness is not an obsession about female beauty but an obsession about female obedience."
~ Naomi Wolf

NAKED ATONEMENT

Darling Body,
Whole Body,
The parts so often unnamed/untouched/avoided
are all parts of you
the backfat,
the double chin,
the upper arm flab,
the rolls,
the stretch,
the calloused feet,
the dimpled thighs all.
I promise to stop letting selfish mouths who do not kiss your belly into our bed.
Let no man bury their shame inside us.
Let no woman whisper her fear into our thighs.
You are not a bank for the discontent of others.
You belong to a bold heart.

I waited until I caught wind of some stranger in Binghamton, NY
throwing their head back under a street lamp
and yelling, "Fat women is sexy!"
before I walked naked through my own apartment in Columbus, OH
and I am sorry for that.
I am sorry for wearing cardigans in the summer to hide my arms
I am sorry for staying half clothed during sex in my own bed
I am sorry for still not buying you that pencil skirt
I need no one's green light to love you but my own
and from here on out it is all emerald brilliance
and go.

You deserve a love letter without a razor blade on the roof of it's mouth
or a file baked into its sweet
one I need not wear bullet proof heavy
and delivered to you dented in with the anger of others,
a love that need not be defiant,
one that can sit with its back to the window unworried.
You are deserving of war cries and soft love both
of gentle hands and unbracing.

For 18 months in the autumn of 1973 John Lennon and Yoko Ono legally separated. This time period is referred to as John's "Lost Weekend"

QUESTIONS FOR YOKO ONO WHEN MY LOVE DECIDES WE NEEDED "A BREAK"

Yoko,
When you pried your clenched throat open
one word at a time
and told him it was okay to go,
did you know he would come back?
Was it a gospel knowledge or a gamble you had to let everything ride on?
When the time came were doors slammed?
Or did you walk him to an idling car and kiss his mouth sweet as any other day?
Were there nights you wish you had devoured his whole mouth instead?
How long until you stopped puzzling over the way your keys fit into this empty
    house's locks?
How long was your heart a flickering porch light for him?
Did you feel like a fool?
A flickering porch-light-hearted fool?
Did you wonder if they were right about you?
That you deserved this empty?
Did you miss him like a limb
or more like an organ?
Did you dream of his death just to wake up wearing the bed like an oversized shirt?
What about the laundry Yoko?
Did you wash and re-hang his shirts
so they would be perfect upon his return?
Or did you let them fester, take root and bloom
a corpse flower
full of his scent in case he didn't?

Did you sit with your ear to the ground for news?
Did it make your skin roll back in envy
when he seemed so fine without you?
Tell me how you wanted him to fall apart just a little?
Just enough that you could hear him wail your name
with the ankles of his new muse buckled around his waist
Did you fuck just anyone who so much as smelled
different to put a distance greater than miles between your skins,
beg them to sandpaper his fingerprints from your collarbones
handfuls of vengeance and solace pulled greedily from their backs?
Every heavy breath a prayer
that you might love this one better

Every moan proof
that it is not you who is replaceable
that these strangers hands might just touch you correct
enough.
Tell me, how you hated them all just a little?
Punished them all just a little?
Yoko,
When you let him come home again
How?
Did you burn enough candles down to the metal wishing him back?
Or
Did you demand he return to you without his feet?
Teach me how to be a tone deaf siren
and sing my love home again
Tell me how many candles to burn
Teach me how to make him want to stay
Teach me how not to wince every time he leaves the room
Tell me, when do the dreams of his dying stop?
Do the dreams of his dying stop?

Yoko,
in the event that my love does not come home again
tell me how to own this empty
or better still what fills it best
tell me what to do with the indelible fingerprints
should I cast them in bronze?
tell me what to do with the regret of undevored mouths
and careless tongues
Tell me how to scream out this anger so it does not make a war of me
What to do with these new clumsy lovers
and their mis-matched hands
the resentment
the doubt
the self loathing
this foolish still flickering porch light heart
Yoko,
just tell me what to do with the goddamn laundry.

THAT SUMMER

Do you remember Mom,
that summer of your son's growth spurt
that summer his fists grew so hungry for my blood
I thought them heavy swarms of empty-bellied mosquitoes.
That summer
...I learned to swallow my dinner plates whole
...I learned to take the stairs two at a time.
...I learned to both expand and to disappear
a trick perfected by filling the holes he punched into me with food
and hours behind books and unmoving.
...of padlocks
slide locks
hook and eye locks
marking the bedroom door frames like some growth chart of his wrath.
...you were an occupied blur of denial between the front door
and that cocoon you spun for yourself in the top left corner of the house
where you had cable installed and watched with the closed captions on
to be convinced of all you could not hear
as though it did not share a wall with a room that rocked with wood grain fireworks
when the door hinges gave way
again and again
where I choked down my own hands so he would stop seeing any swat threat in me
and leave when he was full
...I dreamed of having no more blood left in me
...you slept so much
That summer that burned hard for nearly 10 years with all the windows shut.

Mom,
Do you remember when I was small
and prone to ear infections
I'd be shaken awake by pain's gravel tongued whisper
and rather than cry out for you
I lay obedient in my own bed
a fitful vagrant of sleep
half dreaming of comfort
while waiting for the sun to bring the stir of you in the hallway
before I could ask you for any soothing?
I was not to disturb your sleep with something so trivial as aching.
This is all I can think to tell you
when you ask why I did not say a word about my brother's vicious hands before now.

WIFE MATERIAL

"Maybe I needed to show him I could cook to prove that I am wife material..."
  ~ Stephanie Smith a blogger who took it as a challenge to make her
  boyfriend 300 Sandwiches in order to "earn" her engagement ring.

Is Wife Material a poly cotton blend that barely breathes
or a spandex denim mix that bend to his whims while still being durable enough to
    take a hit?
Hasn't anyone told you that you are worth more than a dowry of pumpernickel and
    deli meats?
When a punchline to a man's joke ends with a woman in the kitchen
it is nothing short of thin sliced patriarchy served on traditional gender roles
it is a reminder of how far we still haven't come.
Hasn't anyone told you that we got bigger fights
than grasping for rings and the approval of men?
That we are still fighting to own our whole bodies?
That we still struggle under magnified glass ceilings
wielded by men who
burn ants in the sun because they can
That we stay fighting to prove we deserve our shoes
That we stay struggling against girdle tight beauty standards to keep us small and
    controllable.
Hasn't anyone told you that we can own property instead be it?
That we can vote and marry for love now?
If your biggest goal is to be material they will pattern cut you retro apron.

By all means feed your love
feed him sandwiches but not your worth
feed him sandwiches until he is fat bellied and content
and remember that you have the choice not to
remember that you have the choice not to because there were women before you
who swallowed all of the kitchen knives in order to spare your fingers.

BLOOD TONGUE

There is this danger in being black in the wrong place
at the wrong time.
Wrong place: America
Wrong Time: All the Time
The sights though
they aren't on me though
I am watching like a child in the closet during a murder
another murder
another unarmed black boy murdered
another black woman
too black
too late
murdered.
I am blood tongued but alive
my privilege.
I am affected the same way I am black
under known, under skin, under cover
my closet skin, my white face, my privilege
my guilt, my white guilt, my survivor's guilt
my assumed innocence
my "good" hair, my green eyes
my white mother
my white mother tongue
my code switch
my privilege

My black neighborhood, my gentrification
my white friends
my being my own black friends
my being my white friends' only black friend
my off white, my gray area
my race card
my race card tucked into my wallet, king of spades
a photo of my father tucked into my wallet
my black spade father

my 1 drop rule
my safe house skin
my paper bag test
my passing
my unintended passing
my still passing though
my backstage passing to the secret racism show when my white friend says nigger
like no colored ears could hear
my privilege is to hear
my reaction is to scream like there's been another murder
my blood tongue
my privilege
my permission to say nigger
like there's some privilege in saying nigger
my blood tongue
it hates the word nigger
the way it leaves blood spatter across the wall
it looks too much like another murder, my privilege.

THE UNBEARABLE LIKENESS OF BEING
ON OKCUPID *in 5 Haiku*

Join OkCupid
and finally get applause
When you catch the clap

Some men send flowers
I get nothing but dick pics
Bouquets of dick pics

Thanks OkCupid
without you I'd never know
how settling feels.

I'm flattered, really
but NOT into becoming
your 5th sisterwife

Join OkCupid
the ambiance of walmart
but no need for pants!

AN OPEN LETTER TO THE ASSISTANT
MANAGER OF THE KFC I VISITED LAST WEEK

Dear Tammi,
No matter how you dress it up the fact remains
that there are essentially 7 items on your menu
4 of these are chicken
The rest are simply side dishes that people merely tolerate.
So when you tell me, midway thru placing my order,
that you are out of chicken
I cannot help but wonder why the doors are unlocked
Why the sign out front is illuminated?
Why the doors are unlocked
Or why you bothered matching your eye shadow to your shirt and coming into
    work today?
So my choice now is Kentucky or fried?!

I will forgo the hows and whys
and simply remind you that when KFC runs out for chicken
the terrorists win
And by terrorists I of course mean vegans, Tammi.
Do not be surprised when flocks of flat toothed, pale skinned hippies fall upon
    this place, pamphlets in hand
wreaking of patchouli
demanding alfalfa sprouts and bean curds!
Is that what you want Tammi?
Kentucky Fried Curds?!

My suggestion, is that you stop offering me complimentary little bucket parfaits,
turn out the fucking lights
and hunker down for the remainder of your shift, Tammi.
Because an act of blasphemy that leads herbivores into the house of the colonel
is enough to shake him from the dead with nothing to satiate his zombie hunger
but brains
seasoned to perfection
in 11 herbs and spices!
But seeing as you appear to be out of those as well he'll likely just say fuck it
and head down the block to Popeye's.

LOVE LETTER TO MY BODY # 14: BORROW

Dear Body,
There is a man who wants to borrow you tonight.
A man I have given you to before
Before I understood that if you have to be talked into it
you probably never wanted it to begin with.
With a man who claims to know something of your magnificence
but will see you only in the secret of badly lit hotel rooms where he can bury
   some unsaid shame.
Shame does not live here anymore.
I sent him away.

ON THE BUS

On the bus 15 cents short
...4 kids under 5, 1 parent
...dirty band aid stuck to the seat
... working class
...reading Auto Trader
Bus pass makes a great book mark
...chivalry has died with its eyes fixed on a pregnant woman wobble to the back
...take up 2 seats with the shopping which did not pair any fare at all

32 Window Coup
Newspaper Floormats
On the bus headphones on no music
Radio tuned to the man talking to himself one seat over
He's a poet out of context
Radio tuned to a woman
telling her cell phone how she escaped a man with lions for hands

Someone left their bible on the 81 crosstown
Someone's child lost a shoe on the 16 local
At the stop for the #3 a woman asks me if I want to know Jesus
hands me a phone number
I cannot call
Faith involves leaving some doors locked
On the bus smiling woman in bright red lipstick
No teeth

City bus runs on its own time
A pocket watch set to fuck you
On the bus 20 minutes late
...bus missed stop
...this ride brought to you by Absolut Urine
spilled soda sticky in your nostrils courtesy of the drunk passed out in 3 seats
    at once.
On the bus shopping bag umbrella in a downpour
...fanny pack and rolling cart full of cans
...1 trip at a time
Four dollars fifty cents all day
on the bus.

DAYLIGHT

For the 16 year old girl who emailed me because she no longer wants to leave her house

I know so well for the want of hiding:
When I was your same age Joseph Rissi called my home
at 10am on a Saturday
with all the urgency of a Baptist church phone tree bending with bountiful gossip
to make me aware that no one would ever love me
until I whittled myself to something acceptable
I could hear the hunger for my shatter in his concrete mouth
and though I told him to *fuck off*
I still hear his proclamation every time I fall from love.

Let us be absolutely clear my Darling,
there will always be bulls looking to make their china shop of someone else.
I cannot say anything to promise that you will not break under the charge of them
or even of some other heavy and unjust thing
as the world does cradle some hard and angry debts
but you are not meant for hiding.
You, with your soft and glittering
already so much sunset on water brilliance
Wrap yourself around something/anything/everything
you can find to love more than they hate themselves
something/anything/everything you cannot live without
(I swear it does exist just as you do)
pursue it with all the force you can muster
(and I know dear girl the force you can muster)
bulls be damned.

Better still, welcome them in
(your welcome mat smile wear its lips red so well for just this reason)
show them the sharp edges of your broken like a bar fight dare.
In spite of themselves
and whether or not they ever admit it
they will be amazed at the mosaics you make of the pieces they leave you in
they will envy your sparkle and curse their own angry granite bones.
They have no course to manage your beauty,
the way the light shines through your fractures
turns you high watt bone chip kaleidoscope
so bright,
so endlessly bright
(you are so endlessly bright my dear)
like only survival and daylight can be.
So the deal is this;
I will scrape Joseph Rissi's stupid voice from inside of my skull
if you just reach for the door knob
Joseph Rissi is wrong.
The bulls are wrong
We are lov/e/ed/ing/able
We are the daylight
and no one can go on if the day starts hiding.

COERCION

When he keeps trying to steer my chin
towards his lighthouse face
despite my whispered insistence that my lips are not lost ships
He sees fit to flash that charming smile and rescue me still.
He is a sailor he says
and knows these seas well
I remind him that I am a mermaid
and know them deeper.
Its just a kiss, darlin'
and my no slips under my tongue polite as pearls.
It's just another inch of your scales onto land

When I do not boat floor thrash against him
My gasping is taken for excited consent
My skin drying out under his touch for playing hard to get

Mermaids are taught early to kneel on ocean floors
praying for a sailor to win us from the water
and carry us home like a carnival goldfish
to never be frigid
to never be ungrateful for the kindness of a man
who has not trapped us
or tangled us up in nets
who did not even harpoon our lovely flesh.

I swam to his shore curious
smiled even
O, how I smiled right up and even through this crime
a gentle rocking crime I did not recognize
until I woke up with a mistrust for sailors,
my backbone pulled through my skin.

PAPER BABIES

My boyfriend sends me a text that asks,
When we have a daughter, can we name her Marble?
It's not the name
but the when that pulls me to a record scratch stop

2 hours later
My roommate breaks up with his girlfriend
because there was *no point in stretching it out*
He wants kids one day
She does not

2 nights later there is an hour long argument at a party
a bossy girl slams her hands on the table
after I say I would have my tubes tied yesterday if I could
She spits threats that I will change my mind
I don't know how to explain
that I am not in denial
that while there is ache here
it is not her same ache
not the ache of clock hands.

2 weeks later I am in the room
when the strongest person I know
and best friend of 15 years
gives birth to her third child
She tells me how the contractions feel
like a wolf attack from the inside out
by the end there is so much blood I am rifle loaded
and looking for the beast that did this to her.
It takes me nearly a month to hold the baby
When I finally do I sneak a finger into his mouth
and feel around his soft gums for fangs.

2 months later
my period is late for the first time since losing my virginity
My boyfriend and I go to the pharmacy
buy a test
he makes a grand show of telling the cashier
if it's a girl we are naming her Erma
after his grandmother
I ration a little of the blood
I am trying desperately to channel down to my uterus
up to my cheeks
and laugh for the first time the whole week.
He holds me so miraculous that day
that the minus sign almost feels like something was lost.

They don't make Hallmark cards for your first pregnancy scare
There are no showers thrown
for the moment you accept that you are much more wind drift feather
than almighty motherly root
I promise that this is a lonesome garden party
never planned in haste
The guest list
a long gathered hope chest of flower pressed baby names
left to decay in exchange for a different life
One where I can give into simple whims without worry
or send postcards to my grandmother from everywhere she never got to go
or curl up in the selfish abandon my own mother shouted from behind locked
   doors for.

I do like children
but I own
and like owning
breakable things
I am
and like being
the one who breaks them
I do name each piece
Magda
Zora
Finn
Jack
Iris
Adah
There is this knowledge that he and I would make beautiful babies
Winston
He would make a great father
Florence
I would, despite my protests, make a really good mother
Oliver
There are the pregnancy dreams
Ella
There are the holding hands to belly
and wondering what an answer might feel like
Harvey
There is sadness in knowing I will not be that piece of miraculous for him
or with him
There is a strange and unexplainable guilt for wanting none of it.
There is ache here
This I have named Marble.

IN WHICH THE POET LEARNS TO
WAKE UP ALONE

If you insist on dwelling in this notion,
that your love did go away because they could no longer endure the heft of you
I say then let them go.
You may mourn them
and all of the things dreamed but left unplucked between you
you may cry
and rock
and drink
and fuck some stranger every time you forget
or, better still, every time you remember the way their hands pulled at you
    without regret
or judgment
or fear.
The way they perhaps coaxed from you some luxurious bravery
to look yourself naked in the mirror
and smile at the heart it contained and the lust it released
and the wild unabashed melting of all of your body into all of theirs.
You may mourn all of this
But you may not now
you may not ever
stare contemptuous into your soft hips
your rounded stomach
all of your heavy and uneven parts
as though they are a collection of children
who simply would not behave well enough
to make your love stay.
You may not punish your skin with untouching.
There should be no mournful candle lighting,
no forgiveness ritual
as your hips are not some obstacle to overcome
Your rippled and stretched skin are not an off key choir to be endured
Take note from your thighs and the way they embrace one another like
    unshamed love
in this world so scared of touching.
You hold so much warm that you must only be a holiday
and there is no penance
none what so ever to be paid for that.

ACKNOWLEDGEMENTS

"For Nicholas..." and "Conversations with my Father in a Dunk Tank" were published in the fall 2012 issue of *FRiGG Magazine*
"10 Honest Thoughts on Being Loved By a Skinny Boy" was published in the inaugural issue of Australia's *The Canary*
"Coercion" was published in *Drunken Boat 18*
"Purple Hearts" appeared in the July 2014 Edition of *Nailed Magazine's Editor's Choice*

Thanks to William Evans and the Writing Wrongs Family for being my home base and constantly keeping the bar raised and the good work going. Thanks to Hanif Abdurraqib for unknowingly reminding me to be a better person and reminding me how much I love my city. Thanks to Columbus, Ohio for being my city. Thanks to Rachel McKibbens for opening doors and homes and arms and ears, for being the big sister the whole world needs. Thank you to my WM family for being for dismantling all the clown cars and for being a soft place to land all these feelings. Thanks to Denise Jolly for the remarkable Be Beautiful project, for being sassy & fat alongside me and for challenging me to write love notes to my body-many of which inspired so many poems in this book. Thank you to my best friend Desiree Pipenger for staying brass knuckled with me for these last 16 years. Here's to 16 more. Thank you to Austin Rebrook for the crown of lighthouses and the jagged rocks both. Thank you to my family and my friends for your continued cheerleading and love. Thank you to Kevin Burke for believing in this book. Thank you to Ariana Brown for being so amazing and patient with me through the editing process. Thank you to anyone who has reached out to tell me that this work matters to them. You matter to me. All of you.

 *Rachel Wiley is a native of Columbus, Ohio where she lives in an apartment full of hand me downs with her stank-eyed but lovingly possessive cat Clementine. She is a Capital University graduate with a degree in Theater Studies. She is on staff at Writing Wrongs Poetry. She has competed in multiple national poetry slams and toured poetry venues nationwide. She is a body positive activist, a proud feminist. She has previously self-published 4 poetry chapbooks and released 2 CD's. Her work has been featured on* Upworthy *and* The Huffington Post.